BRITISH CAVALRY STANDARDS

Dino Lemonofides

ALMARK PUBLISHING CO. LTD., LONDON

© 1971 Almark Publishing Co. Ltd.
Text and artwork © Dino Lemonofides

All rights reserved. No part of this publication may be reproduced, stored in a retrieval system, or transmitted by any means, electronic, mechanical, or by photo copying without prior permission from the publishers.

First published — November 1971

By the same Author:
BRITISH INFANTRY COLOURS

ISBN 0 85524 050 4 (hard cover edition)
ISBN 0 85524 051 2 (paper covered edition)

Printed in Great Britain by
Vale Press Ltd., Mitcham, Surrey CR4 4HR
for the publishers, Almark Publishing Co. Ltd.,
270 Burlington Road, New Malden,
Surrey, KT3 4NL,
England.

Introduction

THE use of cavalry standards in action was first recorded in two Chinese classics on the art of war, known as 'Sun Tsu' and 'Wu Tgu', written about 500 BC. Later, in the years of Roman military power, the legionary horse bore a square strip of blue cloth fastened and hanging from a cross-bar on a spear. Called the Vexillum, its simple design was the gold initials 'S.P.Q.R.' of the republic.

In the 8th century AD, the Islamic invasion of Spain, which also threatened to over-run Europe, saw the introduction of the side attached flag on the lances of the Arab horse. By the time of the Crusades, in the 11th and 12th centuries, such flags had become universal for military purposes for both horse and foot. The profusion of flags and heraldic designs, which was so much a part of the panoply of the mediaeval battle field, has handed down many terms and the basic form of British cavalry standards carried today.

Cavalry kettledrums were in use in continental armies in the 16th century and were introduced into England by Henry VIII. In the early 19th century the status of the regimental standard in British cavalry had diminished. They were rarely carried in the Peninsula campaign and many regiments of Dragoons and Light Dragoons, which at this time were being converted to Hussars and Lancers, gave up carrying them altogether. Instead these regiments adopted kettledrum banners as their colours and on them displayed their badges and battle honours, so the development and illustration of their design is very much a part of this work. It is interesting to note that all these regiments, long since mechanised and now amalgamated, have reverted back to the use of standards. They are once again proudly carried, displaying many more battle honours than before, but maintaining a link with the traditions of the past.

The general format of this book follows closely that of its companion, *British Infantry Colours*; for the sake of clarity, however, the coloured illustrations have not been kept at 54 mm as cavalry standards were relatively smaller than infantry colours. Again, for the same reason, the heavy background pattern of damask silk which is a feature of many standards has been omitted. The book covers regular regiments of cavalry from the time of the Restoration and together with its companion volume forms a complete reference, of its type, on the subject of standards and colours of the British Army.

The author would like to record his appreciation to The Royal Scots Dragoon Guards for permission to reproduce the colour plate of their new Standard, also to *The Tank*, Journal of the Royal Tank Regiment, for the loan of photographs and again to *Soldier* magazine for their kind and cheerful help and loan of photographs.

A sergeant of the 14th/20th Kings Hussars with a guidon of the early 19th century still preserved by the regiment. The design has been painted not embroidered which was usual for Light Dragoons.

FRONT COVER: Cornet with the King's Guidon of the 1st Royal Dragoons, 1815.

CONTENTS

Section	Page
Part 1: Standards of the Regular Cavalry	5
Part 2: Standards of the Household Cavalry	26
Part 3: Cavalry Kettle Drum Banners	41
Appendix 1: Sizes of Standards and Guidons	46
Appendix 2: Royal Clothing Warrant, 1768	50
Appendix 3: Line Cavalry Standards, 1768	52
Colour Plates	17, 20, 21, 24, 25, 29, 32

Part 1: Standards of the Regular Cavalry

CAVALRY, or Horse as it was called at the time of the beginnings of the standing army in 1660, inherited the dress and equipment of similar formations which fought the great Civil War. Raised in troops of approximately 60 men, each troop had its own standard called a Cornet, which was also the name given to the standard bearer. Many of the terms and distinctive features of these early flags were themselves a legacy from mediaeval and Tudor times and many have passed down through the years to the present day.

STANDARD, a general term for a flag but more particularly as applied to those carried by mounted troops, was the largest of the various types used in the Middle Ages and, as its name implies, was meant originally to stand rather than be carried. Some of these, because of their size, were fixed on a gibbet and borne into battle on a horse-drawn cart. The Royal Standard of Henry VIII, used to mark the position of the royal tent on campaign, was a vast swallow-tailed flag of over 33 feet. By the time of the reign of Charles I the shape of a standard was established as square or oblong and it was normally only carried by regiments of Horse or heavy cavalry.

GUIDON, is derived from an old French word 'guyd-homme', the name given to the swallow-tailed flags borne on the lances of knights in the field. Knights of superior status who commanded their own troops were allowed to bear the standard; whereas a knight who fought with only his squire and page was considered inferior and flew a guidon. If, by some feat of arms, he came to royal notice, the sovereign could raise his status by cutting off the tails of the guidon and creating the standard. To this day the guidon is considered junior to the standard and in 1660 was carried by dragoons, then no more than mounted infantry. In fact the guidon bearer of dragoons was originally ranked as an Ensign, as in infantry regiments.

CORNET is also derived from the French, 'La Cornette', and was originally the name of the standard of the mounted Lifeguard of the kings of France; then a general name for French cavalry standards and even a unit of cavalry. Though cornet, as the name given to a standard, was discontinued in Britain sometime in the 17th century, it remained as the rank of a junior commissioned officer in cavalry until 1871.

Sizes of standards varied considerably until the beginning of the 18th century but they have always been richer in quality than those of infantry. Border fringes of gold, or silver cord were a very early feature and to sustain the weight of this the standard was made of silk damask of double thickness. Pikestaffs were similar to the tilting lance of mediaeval times and included a metal bar or staple about half way down to which the mounted bearer attached the swivel clasp of the colour belt. The twin cords and tassels of the modern standard also go back to this time.

In *Clarendon's History of the Great Rebel'ion,* first published in 1662, there is a series of drawings depicting the designs of cavalry standards of both Royalist and Parliamentary armies. A first impression is of a wide variety of design, a complete absence of regularity or any form of heraldic device. The second is of the obvious vehemence shown to the opposing

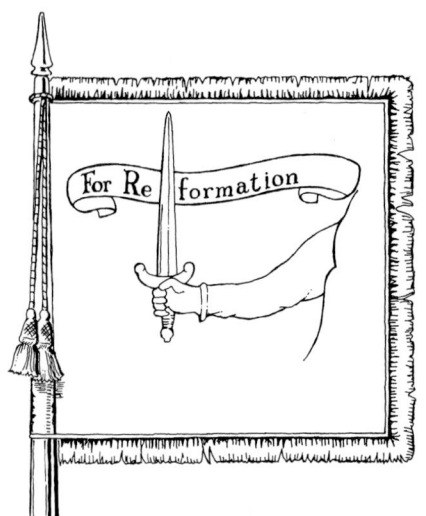

Typical cavalry standards of the Civil War period, c. 1642.

side; nearly all proclaim the justice of their own cause or their trust in providence with a suitable motto, usually in Latin. Undoubtedly these rather fanciful banners are in some degree a mark of the commander's own individuality at a time when hurriedly raised troops fought as small independent units. As the war progressed, cavalry troops began to be regimented together and, although each troop kept its standard, some uniformity in colour or design became inevitable. As an example of this the guidons of a Parliamentary dragoon regiment of six troops are described as follows:

1st or Colonel's Troop:	Plain blue, with silver and blue fringe.
2nd or Lieutenant-Colonel's Troops:	As Colonel's but having the red cross of St. George on a white field in the dexter canton and the motto 'BELLA BEATORUM BELLUM'.
The four Captains' Troops:	As the Lt.-Colonel's but each with a different motto.

It is interesting to note the similarity in design to an infantry regiment of this period (dragoons then fought as mounted infantry), and also to observe the absence of Major as a rank, which was usual in early cavalry regiments.

1660-1684

With the return of Charles II and the monarchy, the army of the Commonwealth began to be disbanded and would probably have disappeared completely had it not been for the threat to the throne by the Fifth Monarchy Men in 1661. It was decided that some sort of personal guard for the king was essential and the present Household Cavalry dates its beginning from January 26, 1661. For ease of reference these regiments' standards, drum and trumpet banners are described in Part 2.

By 1684 a standing army was now well established and at a review held on Putney Heath on October 1st of that year, a certain Nathan Brooks wrote an account which includes a description of the standards of the cavalry present.

Apart from those regiments which eventually became the Household Cavalry, one other regiment which survived until recently was 'The King's Own Royal Regiment of Dragoons' (later 1st or Royal Dragoons) commanded by John Churchill. The six Troop standards, described as 'colours' but probably of guidon shape, were all crimson. The Colonel's troop guidon was distinguished with the royal cypher, and the Lieutenant-Colonel's by the rays of sun issuing out of a cloud. The remaining four Captains' troop guidons each bore respectively: the top of a beacon with flames; two silver ostrich feathers; a rose and pomegranate halved with green stalk and leaves and a phoenix in flames. All these badges, heraldic in origin, had the crown above and were exactly similar to the company badges also granted to the regiments of Foot Guards at about this time. These latter are described in detail in *British Infantry Colours*.

The reign of James II was a comparatively short one but yields more contemporary information on the design of army standards of this period than is to be found for the next 60 years. The main source of this information is Francis Sandford's *Description of the Coronation of James II* in 1685, in which the sizes of cavalry standards are also given for the first time. This is backed by the now famous collection of water colour drawings compiled between October 1685 and May 1686 and now kept in the Royal Library at Windsor Castle.

The regiments of Horse, which later became Dragoon Guards, were composed of two squadrons, each of three troops with one standard per troop; the 'Windsor Colour Book' shows only three standards of each regiment, however. The sizes given by Sandford were 2 ft. 6 inches flying and 2 ft. 3 inches on the staff.

'The Queen Majesty's Regiment of Horse' (1st Dragoon Guards), commanded by Sir John La Nere or Lanier, had a Colonel's standard of yellow silk damask with gold and black fringes and tassels, in the centre the Queen's cypher MBER interlaced in gold was surmounted by the crown. The Lt.-Colonel's and Captain's standards were exactly the same.

'The Earl of Peterborrow's Regiment of Horse' (2nd Dragoon Guards) had standards of plain white silk damask without any design, and silver and yellow fringes and tassels.

'The Earl of Plymouth's Regiment of Horse' (3rd Dragoon Guards) had a standard in plain green silk damask, fringed and tasselled green and silver.

'The Earl of Thanet's Regiment of Horse' (disbanded in 1690) had a Colonel's standard of blue silk damask, fringed and tasselled silver and blue. In the centre was the crest of the Tufton family, a silver sea lion sejeant on a heraldic wreath of black and silver surmounted by an Earl's coronet. The remaining standards were the same basic blue and silver, the Lt.-Colonel's quite plain while the Captain's had the Roman numeral I in the upper corner near the pole. In all probability, the remaining troop standards were numbered II, III and IV.

'The Earl of Arran's Regiment of Horse' (4th Dragoon Guards) had a Colonel's standard in white silk damask with crimson and gold tassels and fringes. In the centre was the Hamilton crest, an oak tree on a green mount with a saw cutting through the trunk. This device was on a heraldic wreath of silver and red, the whole surmounted by a silver scroll with the motto 'Through'. The remaining standards were plain white.

'The Earl of Shrewsbury's Regiment of Horse' (5th Dragoon Guards) had a Colonel's standard of yellow silk damask with fringe and tassels silver and yellow. In the centre was a silver lion rampant, the charge on the coat armour of the Talbot family. The other standards were plain yellow.

'The Princess Ann of Denmark's Regiment of Horse' (disbanded 1692) was commanded by the Earl of Scarsdale; the Colonel's standard was crimson silk damask with crimson and gold fringe and tassels. In the centre was the Princess's cypher PAD in gold surmounted by her coronet. The Lt.-Colonel's and Captain's standards were exactly the same.

'The Queen Dowager's Regiment of Horse' (6th Dragoon Guards) had three standards of the same pattern, green silk damask with green

The Standard of the 1st King's Dragoon Guards being paraded for the last time at Tidworth in 1958 before the amalgamation with the Queen's Bays to form the Queen's Dragoon Guards.

and gold fringes and tassels. In the centre was the cypher, two large C's interlaced, surmounted by a crown.

Details of the guidons of the Royal Regiment of Dragoons (1st Royal Dragoons), already mentioned, are also given, now a regiment of 8 troops. Basically the unusual distinction of each Troop being granted its own royal badge is retained but some of these have been changed. The 'Windsor Colour Book' shows these as:

    Colonel's: The late King's (Charles II) cypher, two gold C's interlaced.
    Lt.-Colonel's: A gold escarbuncle.
    1st Captain's: Two silver ostrich feathers diagonally crossed.
    2nd Captain's: Rose and pomegranate halved with green stalk and leaves.
    3rd Captain's: The rays of the sun issuing from a cloud.
    4th Captain's: The top of a beacon with flames.
    5th Captain's: A tiger passant guardant on a green mount with flames of fire emitting from mouth and ears.
    6th Captain's: A phoenix in flames.

Two other regiments of dragoons are also listed which eventually reached permanence. 'The Queen's Majesty's Regiment of Dragoons' (3rd Hussars) had the first three guidons shown, the Colonel's pinkish-crimson damask with the Queen's cypher MBER in gold with crown above, fringe and tassels in pink and gold. The Lt.-Colonel's was precisely the same but the 1st Captain's was without the cypher.

'The Princess Ann of Denmark's Regiment of Dragoons' (4th Hussars) was commanded by John Berkeley, Esq, and had all three guidons in plain yellow damask with silver and yellow fringes and tassels without any device or mark of distinction.

Several other regiments of Horse existed in the last years of the reign of James II but they were all disbanded by William III. As they were only partially equipped no record is left of their standards.

The standards of one other regiment of dragoons, raised in 1681, as the Royal Scots Dragoons and which later became the Royal Scots Greys, are also missing from the 'Windsor Colour Book.' At this time this corps was under the Scottish establishment and did not effectively join the British Army until 1694.

1688-1743

The general expansion of the army over this period saw the raising of several new cavalry regiments which eventually established many of those descended to this day. Under William III, Scotland raised several independent troops which were finally regimented and later became the 7th and 8th Dragoons (7th Queen's Own Hussars and 8th King's Royal Irish Hussars). During the 1689 campaign in Ireland, the town of Inniskilling became the birthplace of two regiments of dragoons which became the 5th and 6th Dragoons (5th Royal Irish Lancers and the 6th Inniskilling Dragoons).

By about 1706 the dragoons were fulfilling the role of light cavalry and not, as previously, just as mounted infantry, although the musket or carbine rather than the sword was still the dragoon's battle weapon.

It is surprising, however, that for all this expansion and general

The new Guidon and mounted escort of the Royal Hussars (Prince of Wales's Own) during the amalgamation parade of the 10th Royal Hussars and the 11th Hussars on Balaclava Day, October 25, 1969.

concern with the army, particularly in the period of the Marlborough Wars, so little in the way of precise information regarding the cavalry's standards has been left to us. Without doubt, as with the infantry, the Colonel's influence and decision on such matters as uniform and equipment was paramount. Though the basic pattern of standard, as already described, would have been maintained, some personal emblem or device of the commander would sure to have been included.

The standards and guidons of those cavalry regiments which were already associated with the Royal House, i.e., The King's Regiment of Horse, 1st or Royal Dragoons, Queen's Regiment of Dragoons, etc, generally remained unaltered; though the form of the Royal Cypher and of the motto were changed with succeeding reigns.

THE REGULATIONS OF 1747, 1751 AND 1768

The Clothing Regulations of 1747 which completely altered the regimental colours of the infantry also included new regulations for the standards of cavalry and reads as follows:

'The Standards and Guidons of the Dragoon Guards and the Standards of the Regimental Horse, to be of Damask, embroidered and fringed with Gold or Silver.

'The Guidons of the Regiments or Dragoons to be of Silk. The Tassels and Cords of the whole to be of Crimson Silk and Gold mixed. The size of the Guidons and Standards and the length of the Lance to be as those of the Horse and Horse Grenadier Guards.

'The King's or first Standard or Guidon of each Regiment to be Crimson, with the Rose and Thistle conjoined, and Crown over them in the Centre: His Majesty's Motto, "Dieu et mon Droit", underneath; The White Horse in a Compartment in the first and fourth corners; and the Rank of the Regiment in Gold or Silver Characters on a Ground of the same Colour as the Facings of the Regiment in a Compartment in the second and third Corners.

'The second and third Standard and Guidon of each Corps to be of the Colour of the Facings of the Regiment, with the Badge of the Regiment in the Centre, or the Rank of the Regiment in Gold or Silver Roman Characters, on a crimson Ground, within a Wreath of Roses and Thistles on the same Stalk, the Motto of the Regiment underneath; The White Horse, on a red Ground to be in the first and fourth Compartments. The distinction of the third Standard or Guidon to be a Figure 3 on a circular ground of Red underneath the Motto. Those Corps which have any particular badge are to carry it in the centre of their second and third Standard or Guidon, with the Rank of the Regiment on a red Ground within a small Wreath of Roses and Thistles in the second and third Corner.'

The details given in these regulations now established the design and colour of cavalry standards and to a great extent these still apply today. Although written in the style of the time they are clear and simply put, but one or two points, as they relate to particular regiments, can be clarified.

Specific mention is made in the opening line to 'The Standards and Guidons of Dragoon Guards . . .' and is referring to a new title for a British cavalry regiment. The expense of having to put down the Scottish rebellion of 1745 required some economy on the part of the government and in 1746 three regiments of Horse were reduced to the status of dragoons. To soften the blow they were given the imposing title of Dragoon Guards and allowed to bear the standard as an ex-regiment of Horse and a guidon as a new regiment of dragoons. In 1788 the remaining four regiments of Horse were also designated Dragoon Guards.

Further mention of Horse and Horse Grenadier Guards on the subject of the size of standards, refers to the Royal Horse (later Life Guards). Horse Grenadier Guards were a special and short lived regiment and details of their standards are covered in Part 2.

The new pattern of standard given in the regulation did not come into use very rapidly. From the details given in the inspection returns of 1750 many regiments were still unsure about the design that their regimental standards should take.

When the warrant of July 1st 1751 was issued the part applying to cavalry was a repetition of the 1747 Regulations but it was accompanied by a schedule, or 'General View' as it was called, giving the fullest detail of the badges, devices and mottoes of each individual regiment.

The Royal Warrant of December 1768 is again similar but also gives for the first time the sizes of standards as follows:

'The Lance of the Standards and Guidons (except those of the Light Dragoons) to be nine feet long (Spear and Ferril included). The Flag of the Standard to be two feet five inches wide without the Fringe, and two feet three inches on the Lance. That of the Guidons to be three feet five inches, to the end of the slit of the Swallow-tail and two feet three inches on the Lance. Those of the Light Dragoons to be of a smaller size.'

The schedule or 'General View' is brought up to date to include the new corps of Light Dragoons; the first being the 15th (later Hussars),

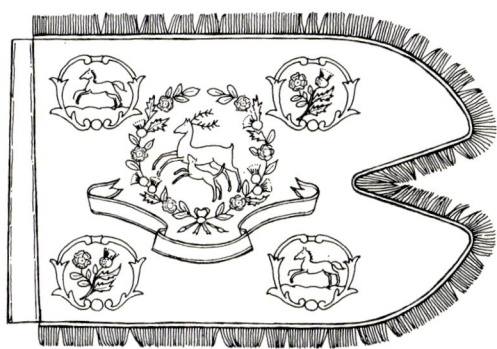

LEFT: Cornet of 15th Light Dragoons, 1768, with guidon as described in text immediately below. RIGHT: Two other typical light dragoon guidons of 1768 showing the swallow tail shape.

raised in 1759. It is also to this regiment that the Warrant authorised the motto 'EMSDORF' and, as such, is the earliest instance of the grant of a battle honour in the form of the name of the action.

No actual dimensions of Light Dragoon guidons were ever given. The one known example of this period, that of the 21st Regiment of Light Dragoons or Royal Foresters which existed from 1760 to 1763 is given as 2 ft. 10 inches × 2 ft. 4 inches deep, both dimensions included the fringe of about 2 inches. Initially, Light Dragoon guidons had the usual rounded ends but in 1768 were authorised to use the swallow-tailed shape, that is a guidon with distinct pointed ends.

1770-1834

The next sixty years saw great activity in the army in general with wars in America, India and the great struggle against Napoleon in Europe.

The success of Light Dragoons in the Seven Years War of 1756-1763 brought about the raising of several more such regiments and also the conversion of established dragoon regiments. Many of these were disbanded, renumbered, yet raised again in the fickle political climate of the time.

The number of standards carried by cavalry regiments during the latter part of the 18th century varied considerably. From a study of the inspection returns, regiments of Horse and Dragoons normally carried two standards/guidons for a complement of not less than six troops; the Royal Horse Guards, 1st Dragoon Guards and 5th Royal Irish Dragoons with nine troops, had three. The newly raised 15th Light Dragoons had three guidons between six troops in 1767.

In 1778 out of twenty-three cavalry regiments of six troops, five had three standards, the rest only two. The three regiments, already mentioned, with nine troops having three.

Towards the end of the century regiments were increased to an eight troop establishment and in some cases to ten troops. The number of standards was also increased to an average of four per regiment. By 1807, when cavalry strength was at its highest, most regiments had ten troops and five standards and the 1st Dragoon Guards, with its twelve troops had no less than six.

Although, presumably, having the same function as a rallying point in battle, cavalry standards and guidons never had the same respect as infantry colours. As far as is known, none, at this time, were ever consecrated and no particular ceremony attended their presentation. When reduced to mere shreds they were replaced with new ones without comment.

In 1807 four Light Dragoon regiments, the 7th, 10th, 15th, and 18th, were fully converted to Hussars and, although not entirely giving up their standards, they were little used. Incidentally, there is evidence at this time to suggest that more than one Light Dragoon regiment had guidons with rounded ends instead of being swallow-tailed according to the Regulations.

During the war in the Peninsula, cavalry were carrying their standards less and less, and by 1812 hardly any regiment had them in the field. Despite the various artists' impressions depicting cavalry standards in the crowning victory of Waterloo, no single British cavalry regiment, in fact, carried its standards on that day. Indeed, it is doubtful if they were present during the subsequent occupation of France.

In 1816 a further four regiments of Dragoons and Light Dragoons, the 9th, 12th, 16th and 23rd were converted to new regiments of Lancers; the 23rd lasted a year before being disbanded and was replaced by the 19th Light Dragoons. As with the Hussar regiments, the Lancers gave up the use of standards even though not officially ordered to do so.

The final loss of status came when the following order was issued by Horse Guards on November 30, 1822—His Majesty 'has been pleased to command that the standards in cavalry regiments shall be carried in future by troop sergeant majors . . .'.

Ironically, though the basic design had changed hardly at all, except to include the shamrock in the central wreath, the battle honours for the Peninsula and Waterloo campaigns were now being granted to cavalry. It was as though the old soldier had, at last, been awarded his medals only to find he had lost the tunic to hang them on. Honours, usually the name of the action, were displayed on either side of the central badge and two regiments, 1st (Royal) Dragoons and the 2nd Dragoons (Royal Scots Greys), added the eagle badge below the central device in recognition of capturing French Eagle standards at Waterloo.

General Order 12 of 1834 officially abolished the use of standards

LEFT: Cornet of 1st Royal Dragoons with standard, 1835. RIGHT: Regimental and King's standards, 1st Royal Dragoons, 1835.

for light cavalry, thus reducing the standard carrying regiments to the Household Cavalry, the seven regiments of Dragoon Guards and the 1st, 2nd and 6th, Dragoons.

1835-1970

The actual changes in design during the next 135 years were very small and modifications called for in the regulations, except for those of 1858, were only minor.

Generally speaking, cavalry standards have always shown a greater uniformity in interpretation of design than those of infantry. Certainly the warrants are explicit enough on the details of badges and devices to be displayed.

Unfortunately, the same cannot be said regarding the shape or type of flag each regiment was supposed to carry at any particular time. There may have been some confusion over the term 'standard' which applied to all cavalry flags at one time or another; although a study of the various regulations brings one to the conclusion that this designation refers to a square or oblong flag. There is no doubt however, that more than one regiment used a liberal interpretation of this term. The Royal Dragoons, who had always carried the guidon since the time of the Stuarts, are known to have been issued with standards during a brief period, 1820 to 1830, though contrary to all regulations of the time. Some regiments bore both standard and guidon and, as already mentioned, the difference between round-ended guidons and the swallow-tailed type was not always fully adhered to.

In the first regulation of Queen Victoria's reign in 1844, the standards of Dragoon Guards were now authorised to have 'square ends'. In other words these regiments were now to carry standards not guidons.

The First or King's standard or guidon was to be called 'The Royal', a term which lasted until 1892 when it was altered to 'The Queen's'. The Second standard or guidon was also officially called the 'Regimental' for the first time.

Also about this time, the manner of displaying battle honours began to take the now recognised form, and similar to that displayed on the colours of infantry. The name of the action was inscribed in black on a coloured silk scroll, usually yellow. Under the 1844 regulation, these were now to be shown on the regimental standard or guidon only.

During the years 1855 to 1858 there seems to have been a close examination into the whole question of the army's standards and colours and as a result one important change affected those of the cavalry. The Clothing Warrants before 1857 expressly directed Colonel's of regiments to provide standards and guidons for those regiments authorised to carry them. The 'Proprietory System,' as it was called, and which had been gradually dying since the beginning of the 19th century, came to an end in 1855. Thereafter, standards were to be requisitioned, via the Inspector of Regimental Colours and subject to royal approval, from the War Office.

In August 1858 the number of standards or guidons was reduced to one per cavalry regiment. The regulation was put in the following terms:

'Her Majesty has been pleased to approve that regiments of Dragoon Guards and Dragoons henceforth carry but one Standard or Guidon; that the second, third and fourth Standards or Guidons, at present in use, be discontinued and that the authorized badges, devices, distinctions and mottoes be, in future, borne on what is now called the Royal or First Standard or Guidon, in the Dragoon Guards and Dragoons.'

This regulation made every cavalry standard, then in use, obsolete. From now on all cavalry standards and guidons were to be crimson but with the distinctive central design of the ex-regimental standard or guidon. Gradually, new standards of the correct pattern were issued and it is this basic design which remains today.

Another small change, at this time, was the replacement of the spear head on the lance for the present design, the handsome Royal Crest of England.

Small changes in size were authorised for standards in 1873. These became 2 ft 6 inches wide by 2 ft 3 inches on the lance, both dimensions exclusive of the border fringe. These were altered again in 1898 to 2 ft $5\frac{1}{2}$ inches wide by 2 ft 2 inches on the lance and remain the size carried today. Guidons have always been as laid down in 1768.

During the remaining years only the number of battle honours scrolls has added to the appearance of cavalry standards. These have become so numerous that it has become necessary to place a certain number on one side and the remainder on the other. Strictly speaking therefore,

Cornet with the King's Guidon of the 1st Royal Dragoons, 1815.

the later design of cavalry flag is not the same on both sides.

In 1956 the War Office announced that Her Majesty The Queen had authorised all cavalry regiments to carry standards or guidons. Since that date all regiments of Hussars and Lancers have been presented with guidons and in the manner befitting the importance of such occasions.

The fact that Cavalry of the Line are now highly mechanised formations has not affected their privilege of carrying standards. On dismounted parades they are borne in the same manner as formerly, and on mounted

Standard of the 5th Royal Tank Regiment with escort at the Laying-up ceremony. Note the sub-machine gun, the weapon carried by dismounted escorts in tank regiments.

The Standard of the 5th Royal Tank Regiment laid on the altar of the regiment's church, St Peter-upon-Cornhill, London, and the final act in its disbandment, November 16, 1969.

parades they are carried in an armoured car with an escort of two similar vehicles, echeloned in the rear, one on each flank. The pride with which standards and guidons are now displayed on parade leaves one in no doubt of their standing in the regiments concerned.

ROYAL TANK REGIMENT

The Tank Corps was raised, via the 'Heavy Branch, Machine Gun Corps', in the blood and mud of the Great War. It became a 'Royal' regiment in 1923 and the Royal Tank Regiment in 1939.

This regiment carries the square standards first p r e s e n t e d to 1st, 2nd, 3rd, 4th and 5th Royal Tank Regiments by Her Majesty The Queen on October 27, 1960, at a parade held in the garden of

[continued on page 22]

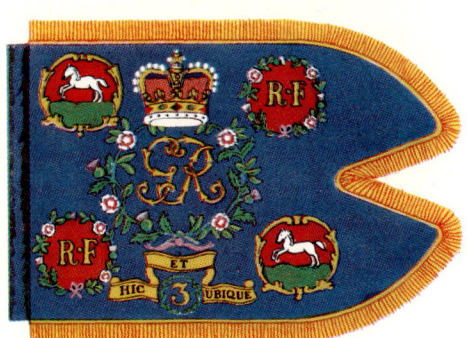

Plate 1

(1) A Squadron Guidon of the 2nd Dragoon Guards on their formation in 1746. (2 and 3) Standard of the 2nd Horse, also known as the Green Irish Horse, in 1750. This regiment became the 5th Regiment of Dragoon Guards in 1788 and a Squadron Guidon of 1790 is shown as figure 3. The swallow-tail ends were unusual for heavy cavalry and normally only seen on the smaller Light Dragoon Guidon. (4) Regimental Guidon of the 21st Light Dragoons or Royal Foresters, raised by the celebrated Marquis of Granby in 1760 but disbanded in 1763. (5) King's Standard of the 1st King's Dragoon Guards, 1906.

6

7

8

9

10

Plate 2

(6) One of four Guidons presented to the 19th Light Dragoons on their return to England in 1807 after distinguished service in India. The Elephant badge was granted to commemorate the part played by the regiment at the battle of Assaye. (7) King's Standard of the 3rd (Prince of Wales's) Dragoon Guards 1914. (8) The First Guidon of the 23rd Light Dragoons 1816. This regiment was raised as the 26th but renumbered 23rd in 1803 and the Guidon was one of three then issued. The battle honours, PENINSULA, TALAVERA and WATERLOO were added in 1816. (9) The Royal Guidon of 1st, Royal Dragoons of 1858. The Eagle of the French 105th Regiment, captured at Waterloo, was granted as a badge in 1838. (10) Standard of the 4th Royal Tank Regiment presented by H.M. The Queen at Buckingham Palace, October 27, 1960.

Buckingham Palace. At the same parade guidons were presented to 40th/41st Royal Tank Regiment (TA).

The standards, all of the same basic design, are made of crimson silk damask with gold and crimson cords, tassels and fringe. The central badge is a Mark I tank of 1916 on a laurel wreath, all embroidered in gold, surrounded by the words 'ROYAL TANK REGIMENT' and surmounted by the crown. Underneath the usual Union Wreath, is a yellow scroll with the regiment's motto in black 'FEAR NAUGHT'. A silver knight's helm on a crimson ground occupy the first and fourth compartments and the rank of each regiment, a Roman numeral above the letters RTR on a black ground, within the small wreaths in the second and third corners. Twenty yellow battle honour scrolls, in two vertical rows of ten, are placed on one side of the standard and a single honour for 'KOREA 1951-53' placed below the central motif on the reverse side.

In November 1969, 5th Royal Tank Regiment was disbanded and its standard formally laid up in the regimental church of St Peter-upon-Cornhill, London. It now hangs on the north wall of the church with the standard bearer's belt, a gift from the City of Leeds.

HONORARY STANDARDS

One cavalry regiment originally had the honour of bearing these special colours. The old 19th Light Dragoons, with the 74th and 78th Highlanders, were granted these by the Honorable East India Company for distinguished service at the Battle of Assaye on September 23, 1803, and a standard was presented the same year.

Unfortunately, the fate of the original Honorary Standard is unknown,

Field-Marshal Sir Gerald Templer presenting the 14th/20th King's Hussars with its first Guidon at Hohne, Germany on June 10, 1961.

OPPOSITE PAGE: Ferret scout car escort for the new Standard of The Royal Scots Dragoon Guards (Carabiniers and Greys). The "vandyk" pattern on the No 1 Dress caps is now yellow, a happy amalgamation of the traditional design and colour of the two old regiments.

but a regulation set of four swallow-tailed guidons was issued to the regiment on its return to England in 1807. The King's or First Guidon was of regulation design whilst the remaining three squadron guidons now bore the badge of the Elephant and the battle honour 'ASSAYE.'

11

12

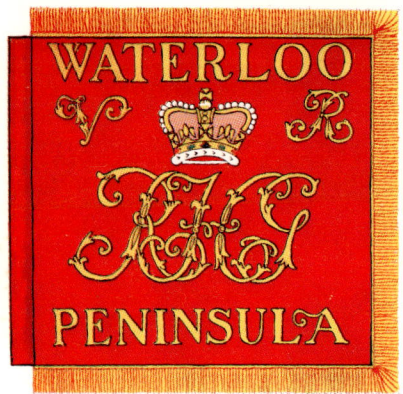

14

13

15

Plate 3: Household Cavalry

(11) The 8th Troop Standard of the Royal Regiment of Horse, 1685. (12) The white Standard of the 2nd Troop of Horse Guards, 1685. The two angels which support the Crown are still to be seen on the design of the Kettle Drum and Trumpet Banners of the Household Cavalry. (13) A Union Badge Guidon of the 2nd Life Guards, c. 1824. (14) The distinctive Monogram or Regimental Standard of the Royal Horse Guards, 1840. (15) A Royal Arms Standard of the Life Guards, 1890. This pattern, which is carried by both regiments of the Household Cavalry, is the Sovereign's Standard.

Plate 4

(16) Drum banner of the 15th King's Hussars, 1882. Modified later to include a further 11 battle honour scrolls but still in use with the 15th/19th The King's Royal Hussars. (17) A banner of the 1st Royal Dragoons, 1890. An unusual feature shows the battle honours embroidered without using a scroll. (18) Drum banner of the 17th (Duke of Cambridge's Own) Lancers of 1904. (19) Drum banner of the 2nd Dragoons, Royal Scots Greys of 1897 although most of the pattern dates before this time. (20) A drum banner of the 2nd Dragoon Guards (Queen's Bays), 1910.

Part 2: Standards of the Household Cavalry

LIKE the regiments of Foot Guards, the Household Cavalry has maintained a certain independence regarding the distribution and design of its regimental standards. However, unlike the Foot Guards, the standards have evolved through many changes, over the last 310 years, including variations in design and the use of both standard and guidon.

1660-1712

When Charles II returned to England in 1660, he was accompanied by a mounted bodyguard composed mainly of royalist gentlemen who had followed him into exile. Early in the following year this guard was established for the King's protection by Parliament and styled 'Life Guard of Horse' but always known as Horse Guards. It originally consisted of His Majesty's Own Troop, The Queen's Troop and the Duke of Albemarle's Troop. When the Duke died in 1670, the 3rd Troop became the 2nd, The Queen's Troop, whereas, the Queen's Troop became the 3rd Duke of York's Troop.

The standards at this time, according to bills for quantities of materials used in their making, were approximately four times the size of present day standards and carried on lances fifteen feet long.

All standards were of crimson damask with gold fringes and long gold cords and tassels. That of the King's Troop showed the interlocked royal cypher in the centre surmounted with the crown in gold; underneath, a large silver scroll with the motto 'DIEU ET MON DROIT' in black and below this three smaller crowns. These represented the thrones of England, France and Ireland and were a feature of standards of the Life Guards until 1801.

The standard of the 2nd Troop bore the Queen's cypher 'CR,' the two smaller centre A's being the terminal letters of her title in Latin, 'Catherina Regina.' As well as the crown, the scroll displayed the Queen's own motto 'UNA SALUS AMBOBUS' (One hope for both).

The 3rd Troop's standard was really a scaled-down version of the King's but was distinguished by a black silk cord sewn in a scalloped pattern and forming an inner border to the flag.

The origin of the Royal Horse Guards (The Blues), long associated with the Household Cavalry but, in fact, not officially so until 1827, also dates from 1661. This body of horse already existed as one of many

Standard bearer of the King's Troop, Horse Guards, in 1660. For details of the design see drawings on next page.

The designs of the standards of the Life Guard of Horse (Horse Guards) in 1660. LEFT TO RIGHT: King's Troop, Queen's Troop, and Duke of Albermarle's Troop. Detailed descriptions are given on page 26.

Parliamentarian regiments in 1660, it was taken over by the King and called The Royal Regiment of Horse. Commanded by the Earl of Oxford, its distinctive blue livery gave the regiment the nick-name of the 'Oxford Blues.'

The standards of the regiment's eight troops were all crimson, embroidered with gold and silver but no information on their design is known.

In the 1670s the grenadier had come into being in most Continental armies and was now introduced into British infantry regiments as complete companies. The cavalry quickly followed with mounted grenadiers in 1678 and each of the three troops of Horse Guards now had their own troop of Horse Grenadiers.

According to Nathan Brooks' account of the review of the army held on Putney Heath on October 1, 1684, the description of the Horse Guards also mentioned the Grenadier Troops and the use of guidons as well as standards. Presumably, mounted Grenadiers would have held the same status as dragoons, hence the use of the guidon. The design and colour of both standards and guidons were as already described except for the 3rd Troop which were now of yellow damask and with the interlaced cypher 'JDY' (James, Duke of York) and surmounted by a Coronet instead of a crown.

Brooks' Army List also includes the Royal Regiment of Horse (RHG) and provides the first early description of its eight troop standards. The King's Troop bore the badge of the crown; the Colonel's, the royal cypher, and the Major's Troop 'gold streams'—this probably means that the design was the same as the Colonel's but with a gold blaze or 'pile wavy' issuing from the dexter canton. The remaining Captain's or Troop standards each displayed individual badges; first troop—a rose, the second—a thistle, the third—the fleur-de-lys, the fourth—a harp and the fifth—the royal oak. All the standards were crimson of the usual pattern and all badges, etc, except the King's Troop, were surmounted by the crown.

Like the guidons of the Royal Dragoons of this period, the badges have particular royal associations and were similar to those granted to the 1st Foot Guards in 1661. It is also interesting to note the rank of Major, but not Lt-Colonel, in this regiment, which was unusual for early cavalry.

Francis Sandford's *Description of the Coronation of James II* and

21

22

23

24

25

Plate 5

(21) Drum banner of the 16th (The Queen's) Lancers, 1888. (22) Drum banner of the 18th Hussars, 1903. The battle honour BELFAST, though never officially published in the Army List, was carried by this regiment for over 20 years. (23) Drum banner of the 14th (King's) Hussars, 1904. (24) Drum banner of the 6th (Inniskilling) Dragoons, 1907. (25) Drum banner of the 5th (Royal Irish) Lancers. This regiment was re-raised in 1858 as lancers after a lapse of 59 years, and received its kettle drums and banners in 1876.

the information in the book of coloured drawings from the Royal Library, Windsor, give precise details of design and size of standards of the Horse Guards for 1685-86.

The standard and guidon of the 1st Troop was crimson with the royal cypher 'JR' surmounted by the Imperial crown, underneath, the usual

Squadron-Corporal-Major with the Union Standard of the 1st Life Guards in 1895. The Household Cavalry has never used the rank of sergeant, maintaining instead the historic and older term corporal for NCOs

scroll and motto 'DIEU ET MON DROIT' and the three smaller crowns.

The 2nd Troop's standard and guidon were white and of similar design except that the large crown was supported by two angels. This feature has long since disappeared from the standards but is still included on the drum and trumpet banners of both the Life Guards and Royal Horse Guards.

The standard and guidon of the 3rd Troop were exactly the same as the 1st Troop but on yellow damask.

A 4th Troop, raised in 1686 but which only lasted until 1689, also had similar flags but of sky blue.

Although there is no reference to the Royal Regiment of Horse in Sandford's *Description of the Coronation of James II* the standards are detailed in the 'Windsor Colour Book'. Comparing it with the previous list quite a number of changes have been made. The regiment now had nine troops and was also ranked the 1st Horse.

The royal standard of the King's Troop had, in its centre, the cypher 'JR' with the crown above in gold and across the top a silver scroll with the motto 'DIEU ET MON DROIT'. Below the cypher was added three smaller crowns, as on the standards of the Horse Guards.

The remaining troops were as follows:

    Colonel's : The Royal Crest in gold, a crowned lion standing on a crown.
    Lt-Colonel's : A red Tudor rose with a white centre.
    1st Captain : The Thistle of Scotland.
    2nd Captain : A Fleur-de-Lys of France.
    3rd Captain : The harp of Ireland.
    4th Cpatain : The Royal Oak. A green oak tree on a green mount, in the branches, the head of Charles II.
    5th Captain : A portcullis with chains hanging from it.
    6th Captain : The red cross of St. George on a white ground within the Garter.

All badges, as usual, were crowned and embroidered on crimson damask.

William III brought his own Life Guard or Gardes du Corps from Holland in his bid for the English throne in 1688. A Scots Troop of Horse Guards, raised in 1662, and later a Scots Troop of Horse Grenadiers became part of the English establishment in 1709. Both these formations were known as 4th Troops of Horse Guards and both used sky blue standards as their distinctive colour. The 4th (Dutch) Troop returned to Holland in 1699.

The royal cypher design, for the standards of the Horse Guards, remained unaltered until 1713, though its form and the motto changed with succeeding reigns. The cypher of William and Mary was an intricate interlaced 'WMR' and the motto 'JE MAINTIENDRAY'. William III dispensed with the 'M' but kept the same motto. Queen Anne's cypher 'AR' was reversed and interlaced with the motto 'SEMPER EADEM'.

From 1696 until 1712, bright green was the distinctive colour of the 3rd Troop which then reverted to yellow.

In 1693 the separate troops of Horse Grenadiers were amalgamated into one regiment. Initially they carried sky blue guidons of contemporary

Plate 6
A fine example of the beauty of the modern cavalry Standard. Presented by HM The Queen to The Royal Scots Dragoon Guards at Holyrood Park, July 2, 1971, the battle honours and badges of the 3rd Carabiniers and Royal Scots Greys have been combined to produce the final design.

design with a silver motto scroll and silver and gold fringes, cords and tassels. The Scots Troop, however, adopted a crimson guidon, but of the same pattern as the English Troops.

It is not certain when the 1st Regiment of Horse (RHG) discontinued the use of individual badges on their troop standards. The King's Troop standard certainly changed, generally to display the royal cypher and motto for each reign as described for the Horse Guards.

1713-1815

This period, which more or less represents the reigns of the first four Georges, also saw many changes in the formation of the Household Cavalry and in the design of their standards. As with the previous section these are given in chronological order.

A major change in design occurred in 1713 and was probably brought about by the political union of England and Scotland in 1707. The royal cypher was replaced by a rose and thistle growing from the same stalk and became known as the Union Badge. The remainder of the standard showed the floral badge surmounted by the crown, over the sovereign's motto on a scroll with the usual three smaller crowns beneath. The use of the Union Badge heralds a traditional design for

BELOW: Standard bearer of 1st Regiment of Horse, 1717, King's Troop. RIGHT, TOP TO BOTTOM: Standards of the 1st or King's Troop, 2nd Troop, and 3rd-9th Troops, 1717.

standards of the Household Cavalry, and with minor changes, survives until the present day. It also preceeds by over 30 years a similar design for cavalry of the Line.

In 1717 the 1st Regiment of Horse (RHG) were still being issued with a standard for each of their nine Troops. For the first time however, the King's Troop displayed the royal arms on its standard whilst the 2nd Troop showed the usual crowned royal cypher. The remaining seven Troops used a rose and thistle issuing from a common stalk with the crown above and the scroll with the motto 'DIEU ET MON DROIT' beneath. All the badges were embroidered in proper colours on crimson damask.

The first of these designs is of particular interest in tracing the evolution of cavalry standards, as the use of the royal arms greatly influences the design of the Household Cavalry standards, as will be seen later.

The two Troops (English and Scots) of Horse Grenadiers were issued with a standard as well as the guidon in 1730. This brought them into line with the Horse Guards and, until their disbandment, generally followed suit in all aspects of standard design and size.

The 1st Regiment of Horse (RHG) was reorganised into three squadrons in 1732 and reduced the number of standards to one per squadron. The 1st used the Royal Arms standard, the 2nd the Royal Cypher standard, and the 3rd Squadron the Union Badge standard. Illustrations of these three standards are given in another colour book, kept in the Royal Library at Windsor, dated 1746. The accompanying description is given for 'The Standard of His Majesty's Royal Regim.t. of Horse Guards, Blew' (*sic*) and are exactly as already described. The Union Badge standard has no scroll or motto, verified by the remains of one, dating from this time, now preserved in the Household Cavalry Museum, Windsor.

The 3rd and 4th Troops of Horse Guards were disbanded in 1746 in the same economy drive which followed the expense of putting down the Jacobite rebellion and created the regiments of Dragoon Guards. In 1748 the white standard and guidon which had distinguished the 2nd Troop since 1685 became sky blue.

The Clothing Regulations of 1747, 1751 and 1768 which completely changed the standards and colours of infantry and cavalry of the Line did not alter those of the Household Troops at all. In the first of these warrants, the sizes of cavalry standards and guidons, and the length of the lance were ordered to be 'as those of the Horse and Horse Grenadier Guards'. But it is not until 1768 that these dimensions are actually given (see Appendix 1).

In 1788 the separate Troop system was abolished, the two Troops of Horse Guards and Horse Grenadiers were replaced by the 1st and 2nd Regiments of Life Guards. For a number of years the old standards were used but a crimson standard and guidon of identical pattern was issued to both regiments in 1791 This was the Union Badge design which now included the Sovereign's initials 'GR'.

A new set of two standards and a guidon to each regiment was issued in 1800, these were originally exactly the same as those of 1791 but subsequently modified. The three small crowns were removed upon the union with Ireland in 1801, and the arrangement of the Union Badge

A Regimental Standard of the Life Guards being paraded at Windsor in 1958. The trumpeter, wearing 1908 pattern service dress, carries both trumpet and bugle.

altered to include the shamrock. The rose was now placed in the centre with the thistle to the left and the shamrock to the right.

In 1803, yet another standard was given to each regiment of Life Guards. This was known as the Sovereign's standard and was identical to the Royal Arms standard then being carried by the Royal Horse Guards.

Changes to the standards of the Royal Horse Guards from 1746 up to the end of the Napoleonic Wars were only minor. In 1758 the 2nd Squadron now carried the Union Badge standard and the 3rd the Royal Cypher pattern. A 4th Squadron was raised in 1794 and adopted a monogrammed 'RHG' design embroidered in gold and surmounted by the crown.

The closer official union with Ireland brought the addition of the shamrock to the Union Badge and small changes to the design of the Royal Arms.

1815-1970

A greater uniformity in the design of the standards for both Life Guards and Royal Horse Guards was gradually evolving. Although their use in Line regiments, was, in many cases, coming to an end, those of the Household Cavalry found an increasing use in the many ceremonial duties. The richness and fine workmanship, always a feature of these standards, also shows a certain simple beauty, to be seen on several examples of this period which still exist.

A completely new set of standards and guidons was presented to both Life Guards and Royal Horse Guards between July 1815 and January 1816. No precise details of their design are recorded but the two standards and two guidons for each regiment of Life Guards and five standards for the Royal Horse Guards all displayed the battle honour 'PENINSULA'. This honour, the first ever to be included on the standards, was embroidered in large Roman capital letters across the base of each flag. Very soon after, the battle honour 'WATERLOO' was added to all 13 standards and guidons, in the same style but across the top of the flag.

Three interesting points of detail are worth noting here. The standards and guidons of the 1st and 2nd Life Guards were always exactly the same. Secondly, battle honours granted to the Household Cavalry were, with one exception, displayed simply as the name of the action. As the number of battle honours increased over the years, necessity reduced the size of lettering and the positioning was altered but the scroll, usual in every other regiment, is never used. Finally, all the standards and guidons of both regiments are crimson. This dates from the formation of the Life Guards in 1788 and has been maintained up to the present day. The one exception to this general rule was the special guidon of the Royal Horse Guards which is described later.

Examples of standards for both Life Guards and Royal Horse Guards of about 1824 to 1840 yield information on the question of design and may also be relevant for those standards issued in 1815.

The Sovereign's standard of the Life Guards shows the Royal Arms in full colour with the royal motto on a scroll underneath. Across the top, the battle honour 'WATERLOO,' and 'PENINSULA' across the base. The Royal Arms is surmounted by the crown and level with this are the letters of the royal cypher GR, one letter on each side.

The remaining standard and both guidons for each regiment of Life Guards shows the Union Badge, with the crown in the centre and battle honours exactly as on the Sovereign's standard: on each side of the floral device, one letter of the cypher and each letter ensigned with a small crown.

The first two of the Royal Horse Guards' four standards are exactly the same as described for the Life Guards

The third standard has the Royal Cypher reversed and interlaced with the battle honours as described: above the cypher the crown, and level with this the letters of the Royal Cypher, one on each side.

The fourth standard is similar in every respect to the third but instead of the elaborate central cypher, a monogrammed and interlaced RHG.

The Life Guards discontinued carrying the guidon after 1824 and from this time were issued with four standards for each of the 1st and 2nd regiments. Apart from the changes in the Royal Cypher the basic design remained unaltered.

In 1832 King William IV presented the Royal Horse Guards with a 'Standard of Honour'. This unusual flag is the only guidon ever carried by the Royal Horse Guards and undoubtedly marked the 'Blues' with particular favour. Made of crimson damask it is richly embroidered in gold with heavy gold fringes, cords and tassels. The central motif is the cypher WR reversed and interlaced and surrounded by six blue scrolls edged and lettered in gold, with the battle honours 'DETTINGEN', 'PENIN-

The Standards, Kettle Drum and Trumpet Banners of The Life Guards, 1896. The Drum and Trumpet Banners are of traditional design which can be traced back to the reign of Charles II.

SULA', 'MINDEN', 'WARBURG', 'WATERLOO' and 'CATEAU'. Above the cypher is the crown and below, the gold monogram 'RHG'. In the first quarter, again embroidered in gold, the Union Badge, in the second and third quarters—the rose of England, and in the fourth quarter—the thistle of Scotland. All the floral emblems are ensigned with a small crown. The finial on the lace is a handsome silver representation of St

Royal Horse Guards "Standard of Honour", 1832. Description is on previous page.

George slaying the dragon.

This guidon, used on ceremonial parade until 1887, is now preserved in the Household Cavalry Museum, Windsor.

Minor changes occur over the next 53 years and are briefly given as follows:

- 1837: With the accession of Queen Victoria, the Arms of Hanover were removed from the Royal Arms.
- 1858: The spearhead finial on the lance was replaced by a gilt three-dimensional Royal Crest of England. The length of the lance was also reduced from 9 ft to 8 ft 6 inches.
- 1863: The issuing of standards to the Household Cavalry was now the responsibility of the War Office.
- 1873: The size of standards changed to 2 ft 6 inches wide by 2 ft 3 inches on the lance (excluding the fringe).

  The lettering of the two battle honours 'PENINSULA' and 'WATERLOO' is greatly reduced and these are now displayed in a single line on the base of the standard.

  The Royal Horse Guards discontinued the use of the Royal Cypher standard. Future issues were made up of Sovereign's standard, two Union Badge standards and the RHG monogram standard.
- 1890: The regulation size of standards changed to 2 ft 5½ inches wide by 2 ft 2 inches on the lance (excluding the fringe). This is the size still carried today.

The basic pattern for standards of the Household Cavalry has remained unchanged since 1890, apart from minor alterations in interpretation of the design to accommodate an increasing number of battle honours. The overall pattern however, has remained the same on both sides of the standard.

The year 1928 saw the amalgamation of the 1st and 2nd Life Guards, but since their standards had always been of the same pattern this did not affect the basic design.

No standards were ever presented during the reigns of Edward VIII

The Standard of the Royal Horse Guards and the Guidon of the Royal (1st) Dragoons are driven past the Colonel during the amalgamation parade of the two regiments on March 31, 1969. The Household Cavalry flag is at half mast as a mark respect for General Eisenhower. The Ferret Scout cars equipped the Royal Horse Guards at this time.

and George VI, but those then in existence were altered to include the correct cypher.

The monogram 'RHG' standard of The Blues was last presented in 1927 and has never been replaced. The two presentations since then, on April 28, 1953, and June 6, 1963, by Her Majesty, The Queen, were of a Sovereign's standard and three Union Badge standards for each regiment.

KETTLE DRUM AND TRUMPET BANNERS

A Kettle Drummer and four Trumpeters were counted on the strength of each Troop of Horse Guards when these were established in 1661. Pictorial evidence exists showing Drummer and Trumpeters at the Coronation of Charles II and though dressed in similar fashion to the rest of the Troop the use of banners for both trumpet and drum is already evident.

From about 1678, special uniforms in the Royal Livery were being worn by the Kettle Drummers and Trumpeters. These musicians were also added to the newly raised Troops of Horse Grenadiers together with certain other regiments. The Royal Regiment of Horse (RHG) probably included a Kettle Drummer from about this time.

These rather grand and richly appointed additions to the regiment were not just used on ceremonial occasions but took an active part in most campaigns. A Kettle Drum banner of the Horse Guards was one of several trophies captured by the French at Landen or Neerwinden in 1693.

The similarity in the dress of Drummers and Trumpeters, and in the pattern of those early banners, with those in use today, is most striking. Even the velvet jockey-style caps, worn by Kettle Drummers and Trumpeters of the Household Cavalry on State occasions, bear a close resemblance to those worn in 1689.

The use of the Royal Arms with its supporters as the basic design for all Kettle Drum and Trumpet banners is another long established tradition. They were always crimson, with the Arms in full colour, richly embroidered in gold and silver and heavily fringed. The only difference, through the years, has been changes in the Royal Cypher and motto, and minor alterations to the Royal Arms. The most interesting part of the design is the two white angels with gold wings, one on each side of the crown, which were at one time a feature of the standards of the 2nd Troop of Horse Guards.

The Kettle Drums of the 4th Queen's Own Hussars, 1907. The yellow drum banners were embroidered with the Royal Arms in proper colours and gold with the battle honour scrolls in red.

Part 3: Cavalry Kettledrum Banners

WITH the lessening of importance of the standard and guidon early in the 19th century, the kettledrum and its banner was gradually re-introduced to fulfill the role of displaying the battle honours of many cavalry regiments.

The period 1850 to the beginning of the First World War saw a great revival in the use and display of these instruments. As with the cavalry flag however, its evolution had already spanned 300 years and it was not just because it happened to be the largest musical instrument on parade that it led the famous mounted bands of this 'golden age'.

Cavalry kettledrums were leading mounted corps d'elite early in the 16th century. Henry VIII was impressed by their use in the French king's mounted bodyguard at the Field of the Cloth of Gold in 1520 and introduced them into England shortly after. The drum banner was added for use with the kettledrums on State occasions and probably owed a great deal of its early design to the trumpet banner which was already well established.

The use of the trumpet in war, in one form or another, goes back as far as war itself. The trumpet banner, like the standard, was designed to form another part of the trappings with which the armoured knight presented himself for tournament or crusade in the medieval times.

Trumpeters and drummers of the 16th and 17th centuries were more than just musicians. Their particular duties in war were to act as emissaries in the field when the parley under a flag of truce was quite a usual occurrence. It needed men of special ability and a certain social standing for this task, which was similar to the part performed by the herald in earlier times. A military writer, at the end of the reign of Henry VIII, describes such a man to be, 'faithful, secret and ingenious, of able personage to use their instruments to summon the forts and towns, and conduct divers messages which of necessity requireth language'.

At the time of the Civil War in England, Major Elton in his treatise on the Art of War, writes of a cavalry kettledrummer in particular as 'a man of deportment, and a politic, discreet and cunning person'. To mark him out, and as a badge of his authority, his drums bore banners with the armorial devices of the General in Command or the national emblem of the side for which he was fighting. In the armies of both Fairfax and the King, kettledrums were part of the insignia of royalty and of the nobility.

Attached to an early Warrant dealing specifically with drums, dated

Kettle Drums of the 9th (Queen's Royal) Lancers 1895. The banners were dark blue and the design embroidered in gold.

1631 and still preserved at the Royal Military School of Music, Kneller Hall, is a regulation for drum banners. This reads, 'They shall be of the colour of the facing of the regiment, the badge of the regiment or its rank in the centre, the depth to be 3 ft. 6 in. and the length 4 ft. 8 in., exclusive of the fringe'.

Recognising its standing in the equipment of mounted troops it is not surprising that with the Restoration, both Horse Guards and the Royal Regiment of Horse were issued with kettledrums and banners; but for many years these were the only regiments who were allowed to use them.

An interesting illustration survives in Sandford's engravings of the Coronation of James II in 1685. A small pair of kettledrums, or 'Nakers' as they were called, are shown carried on the back of a drummer boy; a single pace behind marches the drummer, energetically beating as they go. Apparently, these dismounted kettledrums were used for very many years and a similar scene is also depicted in a scroll of the wedding of Queen Victoria in 1840.

During the early years of the reign of Charles II, the position of intermediary once held by the kettledrummer appears to have lapsed. This role was entirely taken over by the trumpeter and it was he who accompanied the white flag of truce; unlike the kettledrummer, he was now counted as an non-combatant. There is also much evidence which shows that from about 1680, and for some time to come, negro slaves were brought and trained as kettledrummers and trumpeters in both Household and Line regiments.

In 1678, The Queen Majesty's Regiment of Horse, later 1st Dragoon Guards, were allowed a kettledrummer as well as seven trumpeters. All the banners were crimson with gold and silver fringes, strings and tassels and embroidered with the Royal Arms. This was changed in 1692 when the banners of crimson damask were embroidered with the crown and cypher of William and Mary, the fringes silver and crimson.

The written evidence on the subject of which cavalry regiments had kettledrums in the early 18th century is very conflicting. It is generally accepted however, that this privilege, granted only by the sovereign, was restricted to a few regiments of Horse, those which were later known as Dragoon Guards. A document entitled 'The Establishment of H.M. Guards, Garrisons and Land Forces' dated December 25, 1735, gives a list of those regiments in which a kettledrummer was counted on the strength. This included one to each of the four Troops of Horse Guards (Life Guards), one to H.M. Royal Regiment of Horse (RHG Blues), one to H.M. Own Regiment of Horse (1st Dragoon Guards) and one to each of two other unnamed regiments of Horse. The Horse Grenadier Guards and the eight regiments of Dragoons had neither kettledrums nor trumpets, but were equipped with hautbois and side drums. The hautbois was a woodwind instrument rather like the belled clarinet but sounding like a very loud oboe (which is in fact its modern derivative). It was a popular instrument in both mounted and foot regiments of the army, hautboy was also a rank equivalent to bandsman.

The document of 1735 is in itself misleading since the practice of allowing cavalry regiments to use kettledrums captured from the enemy battle certainly applied to at least one regiment of Dragoons before this date. This custom, long recognised in Continental armies and later encouraged during the reigns of George I and George II, seems to have started during the Marlborough campaigns. Kettledrums were listed together with standards and cannon as trophies won from the French at the battle of Blenheim.

Chronologically the first British regiment to claim the privilege of battle kettledrums was the Royal Irish Regiment of Dragoons, later the 5th Lancers. It was for its good conduct at the battle of Hochstat in 1704 that permission was given for the kettledrums taken from the French to be carried at the head of the regiment. There is further evidence to suggest that two other regiments of Dragoons which later became the Royal Scots Greys and the 3rd Hussars may also have won their kettledrums at about this time.

By the time of the first of the famous Clothing Warrants of 1747, all the regiments of Horse as well as those of Dragoons already mentioned must have had kettledrums. The drum banners of Horse are mentioned in the Warrant and their dimensions are given as 3 ft. 6 in. deep by 4 ft. 8 in. in length, exclusive of the fringe. Kettledrums of this period were standardised at 19 and 21 inches diameter and cost about £10. From these dimensions it would seem that the banners entirely enveloped the instrument.

The later Warrant of 1751 states that 'The Banners of the Kettle Drums and Trumpets to be the colour of the facing of the regiment, with the badge of the Regiment, or its rank, in the centre of the banner of the Kettle Drums, as on the second Standard; the King's Cypher and Crown to be on the banners of the trumpets, with the rank of the regiment in figures underneath'.

This warrant also clearly lays down that Dragoon Guards and Dragoons were to carry brass side drums with the front painted with the colour of the facing of the regiment, on which was to be the badge or rank as before.

The size of trumpet banners had remained at 12 in. in depth and 18 in. in length since before the Civil War, these dimensions are given in the 'Kneller Hall Warrant' of 1631.

Although the 1751 Warrant called for Dragoon Guards and Dragoons to use the side drum, a study of the Inspection Returns given for the period 1753-1804 reveals that more than one regiment of Dragoons were still being issued with kettledrums. For example:

4th Dragoon Guards :	1767 —	1 pair kettledrums.
	1786 —	New drum and trumpet banners.
3rd Dragoons	: 1753 —	Kettledrums and banners received in 1752.
	1768 —	New kettledrum and banners in 1766.
5th Royal Irish Dragoons	: 1769 —	Kettledrums and music.

OPPOSITE: The Kettle Drums of the 17th (Duke of Cambridge's Own) Lancers, c. 1891. The simple design at this time is shown on a very deep blue, almost black, banner edged and fringed in gold. On the central Garter is the regiment's motto DEATH OR GLORY surmounted by the crown and surrounded by a wreath of oak and laurel leaves all in gold. Above the crown is a scroll with the title 17th DCO LANCERS, and dominating the centre of the banner is a large silver skull and crossed bones.

In a special order of 1766, all regiments of Dragoon Guards and Dragoons were authorised to give up carrying drums and confined to using trumpets only. No mention is specifically made as to the type of drum but according to the examples of returns shown above this must have meant only the side drum. What is important however, is that most cavalry regiments maintained their 'bands of music' throughout this period and the Napoleonic War with or without the use of kettledrums and thereby leaving open the possibility of its re-introduction at some future time.

After the rigours of the Peninsula War and the Waterloo campaign, a general feeling of pride for its army swept over Britain. It was a period of decorative uniforms, granting of battle honours and presentation of Colours. It would have seemed unpatriotic of anyone to have questioned the spending of public money on such things which in normal times might even have caused divisions in the government. The cavalry especially revelled in the most superb display of uniforms and equipment ever seen. It was not slow to lavish some of this decoration on its bands, the pride of any regiment and a great incentive in its recruiting.

Gradually the kettledrums, mounted on magnificent horses often the gift of royalty, returned to the cavalry. From about 1850 all mounted regiments were so equipped and these were displayed with richly embroidered banners. Since the demise of the standard and guidon in most regiments, battle honours—the granting of which was at its height—were placed on the drum banners.

Unfortunately, it is beyond the scope of this book to cover the development and many changes in their design from regiment to regiment, but history and the camera has left us many fine illustrations of their individual beauty.

Appendix 1: Sizes of Standards & Guidons

Period and Authority	Size of Standard Width / Depth on Lance	Size of Lance
1768 Clothing Warrant	2 ft 5 in. 2 ft 3 in. (without fringe)	9 ft including spear and ferrule
1873 Queen's Regulations	2 ft 6 in. 2 ft 3 in. (without fringe)	8 ft 6 in. including Royal Crest
1898 Queen's Regulations	2 ft 5½ in. 2 ft 2 in. (without fringe)	8 ft 6 in. including Royal Crest
1936 Clothing Regulations	2 ft 5½ in. 2 ft 2 in. (without fringe)	8 ft 6 in. including Royal Crest

[continued on page 48]

The Kettle Drums of the 3rd King's Own Hussars, 1895. This regiment had the unique distinction of being allowed an extra kettle drummer and drum horse on its strength. The original drums were captured from the French at Dettingen in 1743. The drummer also wears a specially engraved solid silver collar presented to the regiment by Lady Southampton in 1772, wife of the Colonel.

Appendix 1 (continued)

	Size of Guidon		
	Width	Depth on Lance	
1768 Clothing Warrant	3 ft 5 in.	2 ft 3 in. (without fringe)	9 ft including spear and ferrule
1936 Clothing Regulations	3 ft 5 in.	2 ft 3 in. (exclusive of the silk on the pole and fringe)	8 ft 6 in. including Royal Crest

Those of Light Dragoons to be of smaller size.

Outline Templates (to scale)

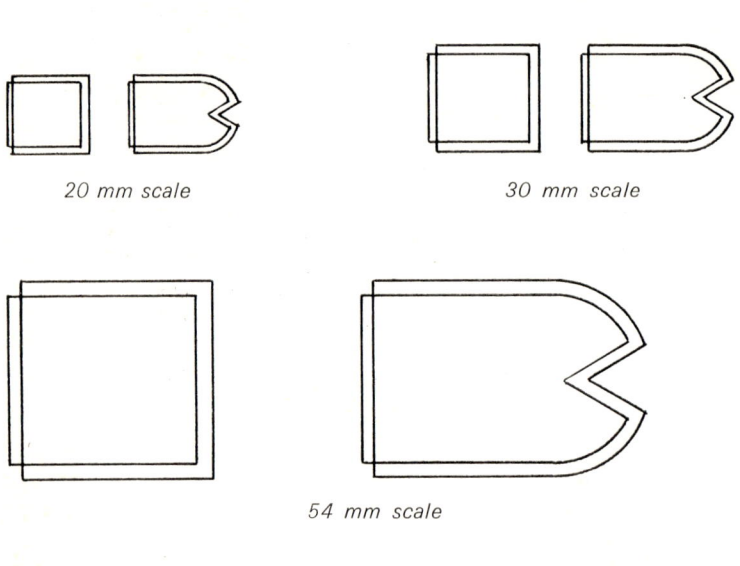

20 mm scale

30 mm scale

54 mm scale

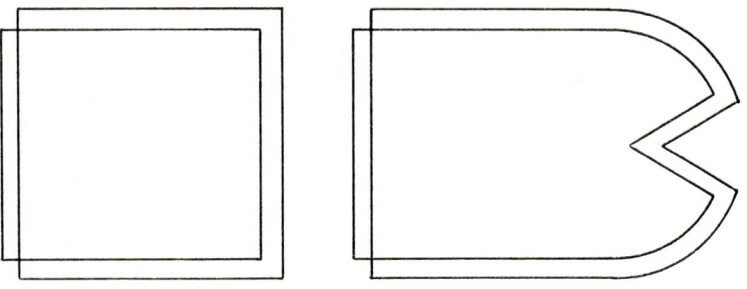

77 mm scale

(Scales given are for standard model soldier sizes)

Kettle Drums of the Royal Scots Greys, 1896. One of the banners is detailed as figure 19, Colour Plate 4 (page 25). The drum horse went by the name of 'Plum Duff' due to its spotty marking when first purchased in 1885, as it grew older it gradually turned completely white. Compare this picture with the kettle drummer of 1971 on page 54.

Appendix 2:

Royal Clothing Warrant of December 1768, George R.

OUR WILL and PLEASURE is, that the following Regulations for the Standards, Guidons, Clothing, &c. of OUR Regiments of DRAGOON GUARDS, HORSE, DRAGOONS and LIGHT DRAGOONS, be duly observed and put in Execution, at such Times as the Particulars are or shall be furnished.

NO Colonel is to put his Arms, Crest, Device, or Livery, on any Part of the Appointments of the Regiment under his Command.

STANDARDS AND GUIDONS

The Standards and Guidons of the Dragoon Guards, and the Standards of the Regiments of Horse, to be of Silk Damask embroidered, and fringed with Gold or Silver. The Guidons of the Regiments of Dragoons, and of the Light Dragoons, to be made of Silk. The Tassels, and Cords of the whole, to be of Crimson Silk and Gold mixed. The Lance of the Standards and Guidons (except those of the Light Dragoons) to be nine Feet long (Spear and Ferril included). The Flag of the Standard to be two Feet five Inches wide without the Fringe and two Feet three Inches on the Lance. That of the Guidons to be three Feet five Inches, to the End of the Slit of the Swallow-Tail, and two Feet three Inches on the Lance. Those of the Light Dragoons to be of a smaller Size.

The King's, or First Standard, or Guidon, of each Regiment, to be Crimson, with the Rose and Thistle conjoined, and Crown over them in the Centre. His Majesty's Motto, Dieu et mon Droit, underneath. The White Horse, in a Compartment, in the First and Fourth Corner; and the Rank of the Regiment, in Gold or Silver Characters, on a Ground of the same Colour as the Facing of the Regiment, in a Compartment, in the Second and Third Corners.

The Second or Third Standard, or Guidon, of each Corps, to be of the Colour of the Facing of the Regiment, with the Badge of the Regiment in the Centre, or the Rank of the Regiment, in Gold or Silver Roman Characters on a Crimson Ground, within a Wreath of Roses and Thistles on the same Stalk. The Motto of the Regiment underneath. The White Horse, on a Red Ground, to be in the First and Fourth Compartments, and the Rose and Thistle conjoined upon a Red Ground, in the Second and Third Compartments. The Distinction of the Third Standard, or Guidon, to be a Figure 3 on a Circular Ground of Red, underneath the Motto.

Those Corps which have any particular Badge, are to carry it in the

Centre of their Second and Third Standard, or Guidon, with the Rank of the Regiment on a Red Ground, within a small Wreath of Roses and Thistles, in the Second and Third Corners; except those of the Prince of Wales's Dragoon Guards, and Light Dragoons. The Rank of those Two Regiments to be under the Plume of Feathers.

BANNERS OF THE REGIMENTS OF HORSE

The Banners of the Kettle-Drums and Trumpets to be of the Colour of the Facing of the Regiment. The Badge of the Regiment, or its Rank, to be in the Centre of the Banner of the Kettle-Drums, as on the Second Standard. The King's Cypher and Crown to be on the Banner of the Trumpets, with Rank of the Regiment in Figures underneath. The Depth of the Kettle-Drum Banners to be three Feet six Inches; the Length, four Feet eight Inches, exclusive of the Fringe. Those of the Trumpets to be twelve Inches in Depth, and eighteen Inches in Length.

TRUMPETS

The Trumpets to be of Brass. The Cords to be Crimson, mixed with the Colour of the Facing of the Regiment. The King's own Regiment of Dragoons, and the Royal Irish, are permitted to continue their Kettle-Drums, and to which they are to have Banners of the same Dimensions, as those which are ordered for the Regiment of Horse.

BELLS OF ARMS

The Bells of Arms to be painted with the Colour of the Facing of the Regiment, upon which is to be the Badge or Rank of the Regiment, as in the Second Guidon.

CAMP COLOURS

The Camp Colours to be of the Colour of the Facing of the Regiment, with the Rank of the Regiment in the Centre. Those of the Horse, to be eighteen Inches square. Those of the Dragoon Guards, Dragoons, and Light Dragoons, to be Swallow-tailed, and to be eighteen Inches long on the Part which is fixed to the Pole. The Poles of the whole to be seven Feet six Inches, long, except those for the Standard and Rear Guards, which are to be nine Feet.

(NB: The above text is reproduced with its original spelling and punctuation.)

Appendix 3:
The Regimental Standards and Guidons of Line Cavalry, 1768

REGIMENTS	STANDARDS AND GUIDONS				
Title of the regiment	Colour of the second or third standard or guidon	Embroidery on the three standards	Fringe on the three standards	Badge or device on the second or third standard or guidon	Motto on the second and third standard or guidon
1st or King's Regt of Dragoon Guards	Blue	Gold	Gold	King's Cypher GR within the Garter	
2nd or Queen's Regt of Dragoon Guards	Buff	Gold	Gold	Queen's Cypher within the Garter	
3rd or Prince of Wales's Regt of Dragoon Guards	White	Gold and Silver	Gold and Silver	Feathers issuing out of a Coronet; a rising sun and red dragon	ICH DIEN
1st Horse	Blue	Gold	Gold	Rank of the Regt IH	
2nd Regt of Horse	Full Green	Gold	Gold	Rank of the Regt IIH	VESTIGIA NULLA RETRORSUM
3rd Regt of Horse, or Carabiniers	White	Gold	Gold	Rank of the Regt IIIH	
4th Regt of Horse	Black	Gold	Gold and Silver	Rank of the Regt IVH	
1st or Royal Dragoons	Blue	Gold	Gold	Crest of England within the Garter	
2nd or Royal North British Dragoons	Blue	Gold and Silver	Gold and Silver	Thistle within the circle of St Andrew	NEMO ME IMPUNE LACESSIT
3rd or King's Own Regt of Dragoons	Blue	Gold	Gold	White horse within the Garter	NEC ASPERA TERRENT
4th Regt of Dragoons	Full Green	Silver	Silver and Blue	Rank of the Regt IVD	
5th or Royal Irish Dragoons	Blue	Gold and Silver	Gold and Silver	Harp and Crown	
6th or the Inniskilling Dragoons	Full Yellow	Silver	Silver and Blue	Castle of Inniskilling	
7th or the Queen's Regt of Dragoons	White	Gold	Gold	Queen's Cypher within the Garter	
8th Regt of Dragoons	Yellow	Silver	Silver and Yellow	Rank of the Regt VIIID	
9th Regt of Dragoons	Buff	Silver	Silver and Blue	Rank of the Regt IXD	
10th Regt of Dragoons	Deep Yellow	Silver	Silver and Green	Rank of the Regt XD	
11th Regt of Dragoons	Buff	Silver	Silver and Green	Rank of the Regt XID	

REGIMENTS	STANDARDS AND GUIDONS				
Title of the regiment	Colour of the second or third standard or guidon	Embroidery on the three standards	Fringe on the three standards	Badge or device on the second or third standard or guidon	Motto on the second and third standard or guidon
12th Regt or Prince of Wales's Light Dragoons	Black	Silver painted	Silver	Feathers issuing out of a Coronet; a rising sun and red dragon	ICH DIEN
13th Regt of Dragoons	Deep Green	Silver	Silver and Yellow	Rank of the Regt XIIID	
14th Regt of Dragoons	Lemon	Silver	Silver and Red	Rank of the Regt XIVD	
15th or King's Light Dragoons	Blue	Gold painted	Gold	King's Crest within the Garter	EMSDORFF
16th or Queen's Light Dragoons	Blue	Gold and Silver painted	Gold	Queen's Cypher within the Garter	AUT CURSU AUT COMINUS ARMIS
17th Regt of Light Dragoons	White	Gold and Silver painted	Silver and Red	Deaths Head	OR GLORY
18th Regt of Light Dragoons	White	Gold and Silver painted	Silver	Rank of the Regt XVIIILD	

OVERLEAF: The splendour and tradition of the past is recalled in modern times by the Kettle Drums of The Royal Scots Dragoon Guards. This picture, taken at the amalgamation parade of two famous regiments in July 1971, features the unique white bearskin cap and one drum banner of both 3rd Carabiniers and The Royal Scots Greys, the two regiments concerned.

Companion Volume

BRITISH INFANTRY COLOURS by Dino Lemonofides

Available in either paperback (card cover) or hardback (casebound with dustjacket) editions.

A splendidly illustrated history of the evolution of the colours of British infantry regiments from 1660 to the present date. In easy-to-follow style, this book provides a superb coverage of a subject only lightly touched on before. A feature is the exquisite draughtsmanship of the colours shown in the seven colour plates—all to 54mm scale for the benefit of model soldier collectors. A very useful feature is an appendix giving a complete listing of all British line infantry regiments with details which include facing colours and re-organisation dates. This book and the present volume are essential additions to the bookshelves of all military enthusiasts.

The Almark Publications list includes many titles of interest to military enthusiasts. A free illustrated catalogue is available from the publishers: Almark Publishing Co. Ltd. 270 Burlington Road, New Malden, Surrey, KT3 4NL.